the Cottage Journal

the Cottage Journal

A PLACE TO RECORD EVERYTHING ABOUT YOUR COTTAGE, CABIN OR CAMP

whitecap

Text provided and edited by Wayne Lennox
Cover photograph by Layne Kennedy/Corbis
Cover and interior design by Jacqui Thomas
Interior illustrations by Art Parts

Printed and bound in Canada

LIBRARY AND ARCHIVES CANADA CATALOGUING IN PUBLICATION

The cottage journal / Wayne Lennox, editor. — 2nd ed.

ISBN 1-55285-666-6

1. Vacation homes. 2. Blank-books. I. Lennox, Wayne

HD7289.2.L45 2005   643'.25   C2005-900612-9

The publisher acknowledges the financial support of the Government of Canada through the Book Publishing Industry Development Program for our publishing activities.

We are committed to protecting the environment and to the responsible use of natural resources. We are acting on this commitment by working with suppliers and printers to phase out our use of paper produced from ancient forests. This book is printed by Friesens on 100% post-consumer recycled paper, processed chlorine free and printed with vegetable-based inks. We are working with Markets Initiative (www.oldgrowthfree.com) on this project.

Contents

Cottage History

Cottage History

ORIGINAL OWNERS _____

DATE COTTAGE BUILT _____

_____

WHO BUILT IT? _____

_____

_____

DETAILS _____

_____

_____

_____

_____

_____

_____

_____

_____

_____

_____

_____

_____

_____

_____

_____

SOLD TO _____ YEAR _____

SOLD TO _____ YEAR _____

SOLD TO _____ YEAR _____

SOLD TO _____ YEAR _____

SOLD TO _____ YEAR _____

SOLD TO _____ YEAR _____

Local Information

Local Directory

OWNER _____

COTTAGE ADDRESS _____
_____

PHONE _____

HOME ADDRESS _____

PHONE _____

WORK ADDRESS _____
_____

PHONE _____

COTTAGE 911 LOCATION _____

FIRE _____ POLICE _____

AMBULANCE _____ POISON CONTROL _____

COTTAGE CONTACTS

MARINA _____ GROCERY _____

DOCTOR _____ ELECTRICIAN _____

TREE REMOVAL SPECIALIST _____ PLUMBER _____

WATER TAXI _____ CONTRACTOR _____

WEATHER _____ SNOWPLOW _____

VIDEO STORE _____ ROAD REPORTS _____

VETERINARIAN _____ COTTAGERS' ASSOCIATION _____

MUNICIPAL OFFICE _____

LOCAL RESTAURANTS _____
_____
_____

OTHER _____
_____

COTTAGE NEIGHBOURS AND FRIENDS

NAME   PHONE NUMBER

_____

_____

_____

_____

_____

_____

_____

_____

_____

_____

_____

_____

_____

_____

_____

_____

DATES TANK PUMPED OUT

DATE   COMMENTS

_____

_____

_____

_____

_____

_____

_____

_____

_____

SEPTIC TANK SERVICE _____

Map of Cottage Area

You may want to draw a map of the local area with your neighbouring cottages marked on it. It may prove useful to guests. Number the cottages on your map if the cottages don't already have numbers.

Instructions for Guests

Getting There

Include mileage (*kilométrage*), driving time, landmarks, and "you've gone too far if." Also include a phone number to call if all these instructions fail.

_____
_____
_____
_____
_____
_____
_____
_____
_____
_____
_____
_____
_____
_____
_____
_____
_____
_____
_____
_____
_____
_____
_____
_____
_____
_____
_____
_____
_____

PHOTOCOPY THIS PAGE

MAP

(For some reason, the worst drawn map can be more useful than the most detailed instructions.)

PHOTOCOPY THIS PAGE

Opening the Cottage

This list is meant to be photocopied for yearly use.

☐ Install water pump and check for leaks—from source to faucets.

☐ Install dock and check for wear, loose boards, nails/screws.

☐ Check roof and eavestroughs.

☐ Check windows and doors.

☐ Clean windows.

☐ Check woodstove/fireplace and chimney (clean if necessary).

☐ Clean up mice droppings—wet clean methods only.

☐ Check condition of trees close to buildings.

☐ Prep boat for summer use; check lights.

☐ Check condition of other watercraft (canoe, kayak, sail boat, seadoo, etc.).

☐ Check condition of water skis, towable toys, tow ropes, life jackets, paddles, etc.

☐ Check that appropriate safety equipment is stowed aboard watercraft.

☐ _____

☐ _____

☐ _____

☐ _____

☐ _____

☐ _____

☐ _____

☐ _____

☐ _____

☐ _____

☐ _____

☐ _____

☐ _____

☐ _____

☐ _____

☐ _____

☐ _____

☐ _____

☐ _____

☐ _____

☐ _____

☐ _____

☐ _____

☐ _____

☐ _____

☐ _____

Closing the Cottage

This list is meant to be photocopied for yearly use.

☐ Remove dock.

☐ Service boat and other powered watercraft as per manuals.

☐ Store canoe, sailboat, boards, etc.

☐ Service ATV.

☐ Service snowmachine and prep for winter.

☐ Turn power off to pump.

☐ Disconnect water lines and drain pump (don't forget drain plug).

☐ Open all faucets.

☐ Add antifreeze (non-toxic) to all traps, toilet(s) and to toilet tank(s).

☐ Drain and service water filters.

☐ Service washing machine (as per manual).

☐ Service dishwasher (as per manual).

☐ Drain water cooler.

☐ Remove perishable food items.

☐ Check oven and microwave.

☐ Empty and clean coffee/tea pots.

☐ Load all remaining liquid foodstuffs and cleaning agents into a plastic bin.

☐ Clean garbage receptacles.

- ☐ Clean eavestroughs.

- ☐ Close and secure all windows and doors.

- ☐ Turn main breaker to off position.

- ☐ _____

- ☐ _____

- ☐ _____

- ☐ _____

- ☐ _____

- ☐ _____

- ☐ _____

- ☐ _____

- ☐ _____

- ☐ _____

- ☐ _____

- ☐ _____

- ☐ _____

- ☐ _____

- ☐ _____

- ☐ _____

- ☐ _____

Boathouse and Dockside Equipment

Post dock rules in boathouse (i.e. no glass, only rubber-soled shoes, no smoking near gas).

WHERE STORED _____
_____
_____

LIFE JACKETS _____
_____
_____

PADDLES _____
_____
_____

FLARES _____
_____
_____

SIDE LIGHTS _____
_____
_____

OTHER _____
_____
_____
_____
_____
_____
_____
_____
_____

BOAT STARTING AND STORING PROCEDURES _____

_____

_____

_____

_____

_____

_____

_____

_____

_____

_____

_____

_____

OIL:GAS MIXTURES

_____ hp outboard: _____: 1   (_____ mL oil to _____ L gas)

_____ hp outboard: _____: 1   (_____ mL oil to _____ L gas)

_____ hp outboard: _____: 1   (_____ mL oil to _____ L gas)

chainsaw: _____: 1   (_____ mL oil to _____ L gas)

lawn mower: _____: 1   (_____ mL oil to _____ L gas)

trimmer: _____: 1   (_____ mL oil to _____ L gas)

fire pump: _____: 1   (_____ mL oil to _____ L gas)

leaf blower: _____: 1   (_____ mL oil to _____ L gas)

_____   _____: 1   (_____ mL oil to _____ L gas)

_____   _____: 1   (_____ mL oil to _____ L gas)

_____   _____: 1   (_____ mL oil to _____ L gas)

_____   _____: 1   (_____ mL oil to _____ L gas)

Protecting Yourself
and the Environment

Cottage Ecology

1. Use only phosphate-free soaps and don't wash in the lake.

2. Keep water usage to a minimum.

3. Don't pour toxic wastes down your drain.

4. Have your septic tank pumped at least every 2 or 3 years to maintain its effectiveness.

5. Preserve natural vegetation around the cottage and especially along the shoreline.

6. Don't spray mosquito insecticide around the cottage. Instead, drain shallow pools of water where mosquitoes breed.

7. Turn off the water heater when you leave the cottage for any duration more than one day.

8. Don't disturb or change the lake bottom.

9. Use only plumber's antifreeze when winterizing your plumbing.

10. Report pollution problems to the Ministry of Environment.

Swimming and Boating Safety

1. Always swim with a buddy.

2. Children should have adult supervision.

3. Check the area for underwater hazards.

4. Don't swim after dark.

5. Don't rely on inflatable aids. Learn how to swim from qualified instructors.

6. Extend your reach with a paddle or line to someone in trouble.

BOATING

1. Be sensible while boating. Stay with the boat if it capsizes.

2. Always wear a life jacket in a boat.

3. Drinking and boating don't mix.

4. Always let someone on shore know where you're going and when you plan to return.

5. Always have spare paddles and emergency flares in the boat.

The Simple Bear Necessities

Bear-proof your cottage:

☐ Keep garbage in garage or shed or in bear-proof containers.

☐ Put garbage out on day of pick-up.

☐ Clean your barbecue.

☐ Remove birdfeeders until November.

☐ No sweets, meat or fish in composter.

☐ Don't leave pet food outdoors.

Black bears are the most common large predators in cottage areas. Here are some facts you should remember:

☐ Avoid approaching a black bear for a better look.

☐ If a bear shows signs of aggression, make as much noise as you can; wave your arms, adopt an aggressive posture.

☐ Never turn and run.

☐ If attacked, don't play dead (the recommended procedure for grizzly attacks); fight back.

☐ Keep a can of bear spray handy, and carry it with you on walks in bear country.

First Aid: A Brief Checklist

I believe it's important for all cottagers to obtain their First Aid Certification, including a wilderness component, before owning a cottage or even if you're a regular cottage guest. The following is a brief checklist, based on guidelines set out by St. John's Ambulance and should be used only as a reminder for those cottagers who have current First Aid Certification. This isn't intended as a replacement for Certification. Remember to have your Basic First Aid Kit nearby and local Fire, Ambulance and Police phone numbers handy in case of any emergency.

a) Attending an unconscious victim

- ☐ Does the victim have an open airway? Use the head tilt/chin lift method to open.

- ☐ Is the victim breathing? Listen while observing chest.

- ☐ Does the victim have a pulse? Feel for one on the carotid artery on the neck.

b) Artificial Respiration (required if unconscious victim not breathing but has a pulse)

- ☐ Head tilt/chin lift.

- ☐ Pinch nose.

- ☐ Take a deep breath and make a seal over victim's mouth (with your own or with an apparatus).

- ☐ Give a slow breath (1 every 5 seconds).

- ☐ Monitor pulse; if pulse stops, administer CPR (see next step).

c) Cardiopulmonary Resuscitation (no pulse and victim not breathing)

- ☐ Find landmark (midpoint on an imaginary line between the two nipples).

- ☐ Administer 15 chest compressions—1½- to 2-inch (3- to 5-cm) depth.

- ☐ Give 2 slow breaths.

- ☐ Continue for four sets of 15:2—about 1 minute.

- ☐ Check pulse.

- ☐ If no pulse, continue with sets of 15:2.

NOTE: *If dealing with a child (1 to 8 years of age) AR is 1 breath every 3 seconds while CPR is 5 compressions to every breath.*

d) Choking

☐ Ask "Are you choking, and can I help?"

☐ If person can speak, breathe or cough, don't interfere but reassure.

☐ Proceed with abdominal thrusts if he/she can't breathe (chest thrusts for pregnant or obese persons).

e) *Wounds and Bleeding*

☐ R...Rest injured person.

☐ E...Elevate injured limb above the level of the heart.

☐ D...Direct pressure to the wound (if severe bleeding, never remove a blood-soaked dressing).

☐ Treat for shock and monitor ABCs.

☐ Don't remove impaled object; apply pressure around it.

☐ If object impaled in eye, cover both eyes to minimize movement.

f) *Shock*

☐ *Symptoms*: pale, clammy skin; irregular breathing; bluish lips, tongue, finger nails; nausea or vomiting; weak, rapid pulse; anxiety; confusion; thirst; dizziness.

☐ Treat injury.

☐ Keep patient warm.

☐ Loosen clothing around neck, chest and waist.

☐ Monitor ABCs and give nothing orally.

g) *Burns*

☐ Don't use lotions or ointments on a burn.

☐ Never break blisters.

☐ Don't remove clothing that is stuck to burned area.

☐ Use only lint-free sterile dressings on a burn.

☐ Treat for shock.

h) Bone and Joint Injuries

☐ R...Rest the injured part.

☐ I... Ice the injury ASAP—15 minutes on, 15 off (don't put ice directly against skin).

☐ C...Compress using a bandage to limit swelling (check circulation every few minutes).

☐ E...Elevate injured part.

i) Fractures

☐ Prevent movement.

☐ Immobilize injured limb above and below fracture site.

☐ If open fracture, cover wound with dressing and support protruding bone.

j) Hypothermia

☐ Prevent further heat loss.

☐ Remove wet clothing and cover victim with something warm and dry (don't rub victim).

☐ Make sure head is well covered.

☐ No alcohol or caffeine drinks.

k) Concussion

☐ *Symptoms:* difficulty seeing properly; severe headache; memory loss; unequal pupil size; seizures; decreasing level of consciousness; changing personality; shallow breathing.

☐ Seek medical help immediately, even if symptoms occur after several days.

l) Poisons

☐ Determine: type (if possible); how poison taken; how much; when.

☐ Immediately call Poison Control Centre and follow first-aid advice.

☐ Never induce vomiting unless directed by Poison Control Centre.

m) Neck and Head Injuries

☐ Suspect neck and/or head injury if victim: found unconscious; fell from a height; was in a car accident; received a blow to head or back; dived into shallow water; has straw-coloured fluid or blood coming from mouth, nose or ears.

☐ *Symptoms:* numbness or tingling in legs or arms; loss of movement; dizziness; drowsiness.

☐ Don't move the victim unless the victim isn't breathing and you need to relocate to administer CPR or for safety reasons.

n) Severe Allergic Reactions

☐ Rest victim.

☐ Help victim take medication if available.

☐ If swelling occurs around neck, apply ice to reduce swelling.

o) Animal Bites

☐ If skin is broken, allow wound to bleed moderately.

☐ Wash with antiseptic soap and apply sterile dressing.

☐ Seek medical attention.

p) Insulin Shock

☐ Give victim sugar or fruit juice.

BASIC FIRST-AID KIT (SUGGESTED)

Adhesive dressing	Fingertip and knuckle bandages
Assorted safety pins	Rolls of adhesive tape
Sterile gauze pads	Rolls of gauze bandage
Compress bandages	Triangular bandages
Splint padding	Assorted wooden splints
Bottle of liquid antiseptic	Assorted sterile butterfly closures
Antiseptic toilettes	Cold packs
Eye wipes	Tube of first-aid cream
Several pairs of latex gloves	Surgical scissors
Tweezers	Pre-made donut-style compression rings
Disinfectant hand soap	First aid booklet

Taking Stock

Clothing, Towels and Bedding

This is the maddening aspect of maintaining two households. Now you know why the rich have servants. *This list is meant to be photocopied for yearly use.*

CLOTHES TO TAKE TO THE COTTAGE

_____

_____

_____

_____

_____

_____

_____

_____

_____

_____

TOWELS AND BEDDING TO TAKE TO THE COTTAGE

TEA TOWELS _____

_____

TOWELS _____

_____

SHEETS _____

_____

BLANKETS _____

_____

OTHER _____

_____

_____

_____

_____

CLOTHES LEFT AT THE COTTAGE

TOWELS AND BEDDING LEFT AT THE COTTAGE

TEA TOWELS

TOWELS

SHEETS

BLANKETS

OTHER

Household Items

ITEM	ON HAND	TO BUY
Light Bulbs		
Fuses		
Batteries		
Tool Kit Items		
First-Aid Kit		
Bug Spray		
Dishwashing Soap		
Laundry Soap		
Paper Towels		
Barbecue Coals and Lighter		
Propane		
Scouring Pads		
Matches		
Water Filters		
Coffee Filters		
Garbage Bags		
Tin Foil		
Plastic Wrap		
Household Cleaner		
Candles		
Writing Paper		
Envelopes		
Stamps		
Scotch Tape		
Masking Tape		
Electrician's Tape		
Pens/Pencils		
Other		

Toiletries and Hygiene

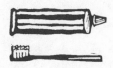

ITEM	ON HAND	TO BUY
Soap		
Shampoo		
Razors/Blades		
Toilet Paper		
Aspirin		
Toothpaste		
Feminine Hygiene Products		
Sunscreen		
Other		

Groceries

ITEM	ON HAND	TO BUY
Baking Powder		
Baking Soda		
Beef Bouillon		
Chicken Bouillon		
Cocoa		
Coffee		
Coffee Whitener		
Cornstarch		
Crackers		
Dry Cereal		
Dry Pasta		
Flour		
Honey		
Jam		
Lemon Juice		
Marshmallows		
Olive Oil		
Popping Corn		
Rice		
Salad Dressings		
Sugar		
Tea		
Vegetable Oil		
Vinegar		
Other		

SPICES

ITEM	ON HAND	TO BUY
Salt		
Pepper		
Basil		
Bay Leaves		
Chili Powder		
Cinnamon		
Garlic		
Marjoram		
Nutmeg		
Oregano		
Parsley		
Rosemary		
Sage		
Tarragon		
Thyme		
Vanilla		
Other		

CONDIMENTS

Barbecue Sauce		
Ketchup		
Mustard		
Relish		
Steak Sauce		
Tabasco Sauce		
Worcestershire Sauce		
Other		

Recreational Supplies

BOOKS

GAMES

CD'S

HOBBY SUPPLIES

SPORT EQUIPMENT

OTHER

Cottage Activities
and Observations

How to Release Fish

Many anglers fish for the "thrill of the catch" and release their fish to allow them to be caught again. If you decide not to keep a particular fish, here are some tips on returning the fish safely to the water:

- *Time is essential,* so quickly play and release the fish. A fish played for too long will be too exhausted to recover. A fish hooked in deep water should be brought up slowly to prevent stress due to pressure and temperature changes.

- *Keep the fish in the water* as much as possible, since fish out of water will suffocate. Don't allow the fish to flop on the ground or on the rocks. Just a few inches of water under a thrashing fish will act as a protective cushion.

- *Gentle handling of the fish* is essential, and hands should be kept wet at all times. Don't put your fingers in the gills or in the eye sockets. Small fish should not be squeezed but should be lifted only by the lower lip. A net is helpful while handling fish, but keep it in the water.

- *Remove hooks quickly* using long-nosed pliers. If the fish is deeply hooked, cut the line and leave the hook in, as it will dissolve. Don't try to tear out hooks.

- *To revive an unconscious fish,* hold it upright in the water heading upstream (if there's a current). Apply artificial respiration by moving the fish forward and backward so that water runs through the gills. It may take a few minutes for the fish to revive. When the fish does begin to struggle, release it.

Preparing Your Fish

Okay, you've landed some keepers, and now you have to clean them. One of the most common ways to clean a fish is to fillet it. Though the procedure is reasonably simple, it does take practice.

1. Lay the fish on a flat work surface (preferably on some clean newspaper). Insert the tip of a sharp thin filleting knife into the dorsal surface just slightly back from the head. Keep the blade as close to the spine as possible.

2. Cut to the rib cage and then back toward the tail, keeping the knife blade parallel to the spine. At the end of the rib cage, push the knife tip through to the anus.

3. Continue to cut through to the end of the tail, keeping the blade flat against the spine.

4. Make a slightly angled incision just behind the gills, cutting through to the spine and rib cage. It should intersect with the initial cut.

5. Lift the corner and carefully cut the fillet away from the rib cage. Keep the knife close to the bones. Note that you'll have to cut through a small row of lateral bones about half way down the rib cage (the neophyte will sometimes mistake these for the main ribs and cut right out through the middle of the fillet); these will be removed later.

6. Once you clear the rib cage, cut the fillet clean of the guts by making an incision down the middle of the belly from the anus.

7. Flip the fish over and repeat the process (this is a bit more challenging, as you have less fish to work with). Hopefully, you will now possess two lovely fillets. In turn, lay each one out, firmly secure the tip, and slide the knife under the flesh and along the inside surface of the skin. You can buy filleting boards, which make this task a good deal easier.

8. If you run your thumb up the centre of the fillet, you'll find that row of lateral bones you cut through in Step 5. Cut this strip out, being careful to remove the bones, but as little flesh as possible.

9. That's it. Wash the fillets and dispose of the carcass.

Fish Tales

SPECIES	CAUGHT BY	SIZE (LENGTH & WEIGHT)	DATE

Natural History Library

There are a great variety of field guides to the natural world on bookstore shelves, but this selection should be the backbone of your cottage library.

WILDFLOWERS

The National Audobon Society field guides separate the flowers mainly by colour, while Newcomb's guide uses a simple 3-point key. Both books are good, but used in conjunction, only the wiliest of wildflowers should evade identification.

- *Field Guide to North American Wildflowers* by the National Audobon Society.
- *Newcomb's Wildflower Guide* by Lawrence Newcomb. Little, Brown & Company Limited.

BIRDS

Roger Tory Peterson's field guides for birding are widely accepted as one of the most reliable birding guide series available. There are other books, such as the National Geographic guide, which some people swear by (incidentally, any oaths sworn by birders on their field guides are binding). Photographic bird guides, while useful as back-up reference books, tend to be rather hopeless in the field.

- *A Field Guide to Western Birds* by Roger Tory Peterson and Virginia Marie Peterson. Houghton Mifflin Company.
- *A Field Guide to the Birds of Eastern and Central North America* by Roger Tory Peterson and Virginia Marie Peterson. Houghton Mifflin Company.
- *National Geographic Field Guide to Birds of North America* by Jon L. Dunn. National Geographic.

WILDLIFE

- Peterson's *A Field Guide to Mammals* by W. H. Burt and R. P. Grossenheider Houghton Mifflin Company.
- *Field Guide to North American Mammals* by the National Audobon Society. Alfred A. Knopf.

TREES

- *Trees in Canada* by J. L. Farrar. Fitzhenry and Whiteside.

Bird Watching

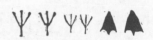

DUCKLIKE BIRDS (MISCELLANEOUS SWIMMERS)

SPECIES	DATE SEEN	WHERE & BY WHOM?

SEA BIRDS, GULLS, ETC. (AERIALISTS)

SPECIES	DATE SEEN	WHERE & BY WHOM?

LONG-LEGGED WADING BIRDS

SPECIES	DATE SEEN	WHERE & BY WHOM?

SMALLER WADING BIRDS

SPECIES	DATE SEEN	WHERE & BY WHOM?

FOWL-LIKE BIRDS

SPECIES	DATE SEEN	WHERE & BY WHOM?

BIRDS OF PREY

SPECIES	DATE SEEN	WHERE & BY WHOM?

NONPASSERINE LAND BIRDS

SPECIES   DATE SEEN   WHERE & BY WHOM?

_____

_____

_____

_____

_____

_____

_____

_____

PASSERINE (PERCHING) BIRDS

SPECIES   DATE SEEN   WHERE & BY WHOM?

_____

_____

_____

_____

_____

_____

_____

_____

ADDITIONAL SPECIES AND ACCIDENTALS (E.G. FROM MEXICO)

SPECIES   DATE SEEN   WHERE & BY WHOM?

_____

_____

_____

_____

_____

_____

_____

_____

ADDITIONAL SPECIES AND ACCIDENTALS (E.G. FROM MEXICO)

SPECIES	DATE SEEN	WHERE & BY WHOM?

Wildlife Records

SPECIES	DATE SEEN	WHERE & BY WHOM?

SPECIES   DATE SEEN   WHERE & BY WHOM?

Wildflower Records

SPECIES	DATE SEEN	WHERE & BY WHOM?

SPECIES	DATE SEEN	WHERE & BY WHOM?

The Berry Patch

WHAT TYPE?   WHERE PICKED?   WHO PICKED?   WHEN?

WHAT TYPE?   WHERE PICKED?   WHO PICKED?   WHEN?

Books Read and
Recommended at the Cottage

TITLE & AUTHOR	DATE	READ BY WHOM?	COMMENTS

TITLE & AUTHOR   DATE   READ BY WHOM?   COMMENTS

Favourite and
Easy Cottage Recipes

RECIPE NAME_____

FEEDS HOW MANY? _____ WHO SUPPLIED IT? _____ WHEN? _____

INGREDIENTS _____

_____

_____

_____

_____

_____

_____

_____

_____

_____

_____

_____

METHOD_____

_____

_____

_____

_____

_____

_____

_____

_____

_____

_____

_____

_____

_____

_____

_____

_____

RECIPE NAME_____

FEEDS HOW MANY? _____WHO SUPPLIED IT? _____WHEN? _____

INGREDIENTS _____

_____

_____

_____

_____

_____

_____

_____

_____

_____

_____

_____

METHOD_____

_____

_____

_____

_____

_____

_____

_____

_____

_____

_____

_____

_____

_____

_____

_____

_____

_____

_____

_____

RECIPE NAME _____

FEEDS HOW MANY? _____ WHO SUPPLIED IT? _____ WHEN? _____

INGREDIENTS _____

_____

_____

_____

_____

_____

_____

_____

_____

_____

METHOD _____

_____

_____

_____

_____

_____

_____

_____

_____

_____

_____

_____

_____

_____

_____

_____

_____

_____

RECIPE NAME

FEEDS HOW MANY? _____ WHO SUPPLIED IT? _____ WHEN? _____

INGREDIENTS

METHOD

RECIPE NAME_____

FEEDS HOW MANY? _____ WHO SUPPLIED IT? _____ WHEN? _____

INGREDIENTS _____

_____

_____

_____

_____

_____

_____

_____

_____

_____

_____

METHOD_____

_____

_____

_____

_____

_____

_____

_____

_____

_____

_____

_____

_____

_____

_____

_____

_____

RECIPE NAME_____

FEEDS HOW MANY? _____ WHO SUPPLIED IT? _____ WHEN? _____

INGREDIENTS _____

_____

_____

_____

_____

_____

_____

_____

_____

_____

_____

METHOD _____

_____

_____

_____

_____

_____

_____

_____

_____

_____

_____

_____

_____

_____

_____

_____

_____

_____

_____

RECIPE NAME_____

FEEDS HOW MANY? _____WHO SUPPLIED IT? _____WHEN? _____

INGREDIENTS _____

_____

_____

_____

_____

_____

_____

_____

_____

METHOD_____

_____

_____

_____

_____

_____

_____

_____

_____

_____

_____

_____

_____

_____

_____

_____

RECIPE NAME_____

FEEDS HOW MANY? _____ WHO SUPPLIED IT? _____ WHEN? _____

INGREDIENTS _____

_____

_____

_____

_____

_____

_____

_____

_____

_____

_____

_____

METHOD_____

_____

_____

_____

_____

_____

_____

_____

_____

_____

_____

_____

_____

_____

_____

_____

_____

_____

_____

RECIPE NAME_____

FEEDS HOW MANY? _____ WHO SUPPLIED IT? _____ WHEN? _____

INGREDIENTS _____

_____

_____

_____

_____

_____

_____

_____

_____

_____

METHOD_____

_____

_____

_____

_____

_____

_____

_____

_____

_____

_____

_____

_____

_____

_____

_____

_____

_____

RECIPE NAME_____

FEEDS HOW MANY? _____WHO SUPPLIED IT? _____WHEN?_____

INGREDIENTS _____

_____

_____

_____

_____

_____

_____

_____

_____

_____

_____

_____

METHOD_____

_____

_____

_____

_____

_____

_____

_____

_____

_____

_____

_____

_____

_____

_____

_____

_____

_____

_____

_____

RECIPE NAME_____

FEEDS HOW MANY? _____WHO SUPPLIED IT? _____WHEN? _____

INGREDIENTS _____

_____
_____
_____
_____
_____
_____
_____
_____
_____

METHOD_____

_____
_____
_____
_____
_____
_____
_____
_____
_____
_____
_____
_____
_____
_____
_____
_____
_____
_____

RECIPE NAME

FEEDS HOW MANY? _____ WHO SUPPLIED IT? _____ WHEN? _____

INGREDIENTS

METHOD

RECIPE NAME_____

FEEDS HOW MANY? _____ WHO SUPPLIED IT? _____ WHEN? _____

INGREDIENTS _____

_____
_____
_____
_____
_____
_____
_____
_____
_____
_____
_____

METHOD_____

_____
_____
_____
_____
_____
_____
_____
_____
_____
_____
_____
_____
_____
_____
_____
_____
_____
_____
_____
_____
_____

RECIPE NAME_____

FEEDS HOW MANY? _____WHO SUPPLIED IT? _____WHEN? _____

INGREDIENTS _____

_____

_____

_____

_____

_____

_____

_____

_____

_____

_____

METHOD_____

_____

_____

_____

_____

_____

_____

_____

_____

_____

_____

_____

_____

_____

_____

_____

_____

Games Record

GAME	PLAYERS	WHEN?	SCORE

GAME	PLAYERS	WHEN?	SCORE

Cottage Projects

PROJECT_____

_____

COST $_____WHO HELPED?_____

DATE COMPLETED_____

PROJECT_____

_____

COST $_____WHO HELPED?_____

DATE COMPLETED_____

PROJECT_____

_____

COST $_____WHO HELPED?_____

DATE COMPLETED_____

PROJECT_____

_____

COST $_____WHO HELPED?_____

DATE COMPLETED_____

PROJECT_____

_____

COST $_____WHO HELPED?_____

DATE COMPLETED_____

PROJECT_____

_____

COST $_____WHO HELPED?_____

DATE COMPLETED_____

PROJECT_____
_____

COST $_____ WHO HELPED? _____
DATE COMPLETED _____

PROJECT_____
_____

COST $_____ WHO HELPED? _____
DATE COMPLETED _____

PROJECT_____
_____

COST $_____ WHO HELPED? _____
DATE COMPLETED _____

PROJECT_____
_____

COST $_____ WHO HELPED? _____
DATE COMPLETED _____

PROJECT_____
_____

COST $_____ WHO HELPED? _____
DATE COMPLETED _____

PROJECT_____
_____

COST $_____ WHO HELPED? _____
DATE COMPLETED _____

Special Photographs/Pictures

Special Photographs / Pictures

Just a place to put special photos or pictures (you know, the ones the kids drew when they were little) or special memories. To personalize the *Cottage Journal* you might consider pasting a picture of your cottage over the photograph on the cover of this journal.

Special Photographs/Pictures

Special Photographs/Pictures

Special Photographs / Pictures

Special Photographs/Pictures

Special Photographs/Pictures

Special Photographs/Pictures

Daily Journal

DATE _____   WEATHER _____
                                          _____

_____
_____
_____
_____
_____
_____
_____
_____
_____
_____
_____
_____
_____

DATE _____   WEATHER _____
                                          _____

_____
_____
_____
_____
_____
_____
_____
_____
_____
_____
_____
_____
_____

DATE _____

WEATHER _____
_____
_____
_____
_____
_____
_____
_____
_____
_____
_____
_____
_____
_____
_____
_____
_____

DATE _____ WEATHER _____
_____
_____
_____
_____
_____
_____
_____
_____
_____
_____
_____
_____
_____
_____
_____
_____

DATE _____ WEATHER _____

_____

_____
_____
_____
_____
_____
_____
_____
_____
_____
_____
_____
_____
_____

DATE _____ WEATHER _____

_____

_____
_____
_____
_____
_____
_____
_____
_____
_____
_____
_____
_____
_____
_____

DATE _____

WEATHER _____

_____

_____

_____

_____

_____

_____

_____

_____

_____

_____

_____

_____

_____

_____

_____

_____

DATE _____   WEATHER _____

_____

_____

_____

_____

_____

_____

_____

_____

_____

_____

_____

_____

_____

_____

_____

_____

_____

_____

DATE _____   WEATHER _____
_____
_____
_____
_____
_____
_____
_____
_____
_____
_____
_____
_____
_____
_____
_____

DATE _____   WEATHER _____
_____
_____
_____
_____
_____
_____
_____
_____
_____
_____
_____
_____
_____
_____
_____

DATE _____

WEATHER _____

_____

_____

_____

_____

_____

_____

_____

_____

_____

_____

_____

_____

_____

_____

_____

DATE _____ WEATHER _____

_____

_____

_____

_____

_____

_____

_____

_____

_____

_____

_____

_____

_____

_____

_____

_____

DATE _____ WEATHER _____
_____
_____
_____
_____
_____
_____
_____
_____
_____
_____
_____
_____
_____
_____
_____
_____
_____

DATE _____ WEATHER _____
_____
_____
_____
_____
_____
_____
_____
_____
_____
_____
_____
_____
_____
_____
_____
_____
_____

DATE _____

WEATHER _____
_____
_____
_____
_____
_____
_____
_____
_____
_____
_____
_____
_____
_____
_____
_____

DATE _____   WEATHER _____
_____
_____
_____
_____
_____
_____
_____
_____
_____
_____
_____
_____
_____
_____
_____
_____

DATE _____ WEATHER _____
_____
_____
_____
_____
_____
_____
_____
_____
_____
_____
_____
_____
_____
_____

DATE _____ WEATHER _____
_____
_____
_____
_____
_____
_____
_____
_____
_____
_____
_____
_____
_____
_____

DATE _____

WEATHER _____
_____
_____
_____
_____
_____
_____
_____
_____
_____
_____
_____
_____
_____
_____
_____

DATE _____ WEATHER _____
_____
_____
_____
_____
_____
_____
_____
_____
_____
_____
_____
_____
_____
_____
_____
_____
_____

DATE _____ WEATHER _____

_____

_____
_____
_____
_____
_____
_____
_____
_____
_____
_____
_____
_____
_____
_____
_____

DATE _____ WEATHER _____

_____

_____
_____
_____
_____
_____
_____
_____
_____
_____
_____
_____
_____
_____
_____
_____

DATE _____

WEATHER _____

_____

_____

_____

_____

_____

_____

_____

_____

_____

_____

_____

_____

_____

_____

_____

DATE _____   WEATHER _____

_____

_____

_____

_____

_____

_____

_____

_____

_____

_____

_____

_____

_____

_____

_____

_____

DATE _____ WEATHER _____
_____
_____
_____
_____
_____
_____
_____
_____
_____
_____
_____
_____
_____
_____
_____

DATE _____ WEATHER _____
_____
_____
_____
_____
_____
_____
_____
_____
_____
_____
_____
_____
_____
_____
_____

DATE _____

WEATHER _____

_____

_____

_____

_____

_____

_____

_____

_____

_____

_____

_____

_____

_____

_____

DATE _____   WEATHER _____

_____

_____

_____

_____

_____

_____

_____

_____

_____

_____

_____

_____

_____

_____

_____

DATE _____ WEATHER _____

_____

_____

_____

_____

_____

_____

_____

_____

_____

_____

_____

_____

_____

_____

DATE _____ WEATHER _____

_____

_____

_____

_____

_____

_____

_____

_____

_____

_____

_____

_____

_____

_____

DATE _____

WEATHER _____

_____

_____

_____

_____

_____

_____

_____

_____

_____

_____

_____

_____

_____

_____

_____

DATE _____   WEATHER _____

_____

_____

_____

_____

_____

_____

_____

_____

_____

_____

_____

_____

_____

_____

_____

DATE _____ WEATHER _____
_____
_____
_____
_____
_____
_____
_____
_____
_____
_____
_____
_____
_____
_____
_____
_____

DATE _____ WEATHER _____
_____
_____
_____
_____
_____
_____
_____
_____
_____
_____
_____
_____
_____
_____
_____
_____

DATE _____

WEATHER _____

_____

_____

_____

_____

_____

_____

_____

_____

_____

_____

_____

_____

_____

_____

_____

DATE _____ WEATHER _____

_____

_____

_____

_____

_____

_____

_____

_____

_____

_____

_____

_____

_____

_____

_____

_____

DATE _____ WEATHER _____
_____
_____
_____
_____
_____
_____
_____
_____
_____
_____
_____
_____
_____
_____

DATE _____ WEATHER _____
_____
_____
_____
_____
_____
_____
_____
_____
_____
_____
_____
_____
_____

DATE _____

WEATHER _____

_____
_____
_____
_____
_____
_____
_____
_____
_____
_____
_____
_____
_____
_____
_____

DATE _____ WEATHER _____

_____
_____
_____
_____
_____
_____
_____
_____
_____
_____
_____
_____
_____
_____
_____
_____

DATE _____ WEATHER _____
_____
_____
_____
_____
_____
_____
_____
_____
_____
_____
_____
_____
_____
_____
_____

DATE _____ WEATHER _____
_____
_____
_____
_____
_____
_____
_____
_____
_____
_____
_____
_____
_____
_____
_____

DATE _____

WEATHER _____

_____

_____

_____

_____

_____

_____

_____

_____

_____

_____

_____

_____

_____

_____

_____

DATE _____ WEATHER _____

_____

_____

_____

_____

_____

_____

_____

_____

_____

_____

_____

_____

_____

_____

_____

DATE _____ WEATHER _____
_____

_____
_____
_____
_____
_____
_____
_____
_____
_____
_____
_____
_____
_____
_____
_____

DATE _____ WEATHER _____
_____

_____
_____
_____
_____
_____
_____
_____
_____
_____
_____
_____
_____
_____
_____

DATE _____

WEATHER _____

_____
_____
_____
_____
_____
_____
_____
_____
_____
_____
_____
_____
_____
_____
_____

DATE _____   WEATHER _____

_____
_____
_____
_____
_____
_____
_____
_____
_____
_____
_____
_____
_____
_____
_____
_____

DATE _____   WEATHER _____

_____
_____
_____
_____
_____
_____
_____
_____
_____
_____
_____
_____
_____
_____
_____
_____

DATE _____   WEATHER _____

_____
_____
_____
_____
_____
_____
_____
_____
_____
_____
_____
_____
_____
_____
_____
_____

DATE _____

WEATHER _____

_____

_____

_____

_____

_____

_____

_____

_____

_____

_____

_____

_____

_____

_____

DATE _____ WEATHER _____

_____

_____

_____

_____

_____

_____

_____

_____

_____

_____

_____

_____

_____

_____

DATE _____ WEATHER _____
_____
_____
_____
_____
_____
_____
_____
_____
_____
_____
_____
_____
_____
_____
_____

DATE _____ WEATHER _____
_____
_____
_____
_____
_____
_____
_____
_____
_____
_____
_____
_____
_____
_____
_____

Guest Registry

Guest Registry

WHO?   WHEN?   COMMENT

WHO?   WHEN?   COMMENT

_____
_____
_____
_____
_____
_____
_____
_____
_____
_____
_____
_____
_____
_____
_____
_____
_____
_____
_____
_____
_____
_____
_____
_____
_____
_____
_____
_____
_____
_____
_____

WHO?   WHEN?   COMMENT

WHO?   WHEN?   COMMENT

_____

_____

_____

_____

_____

_____

_____

_____

_____

_____

_____

_____

_____

_____

_____

_____

_____

_____

_____

_____

_____

_____

_____

_____

_____

_____

WHO?   WHEN?   COMMENT

WHO? WHEN? COMMENT

WHO?   WHEN?   COMMENT

WHO?   WHEN?   COMMENT

WHO?   WHEN?   COMMENT

WHO?   WHEN?   COMMENT

WHO?   WHEN?   COMMENT

WHO?   WHEN?   COMMENT

WHO?　　　　WHEN?　　　COMMENT

WHO?   WHEN?   COMMENT

WHO?   WHEN?   COMMENT

WHO?   WHEN?   COMMENT

WHO?   WHEN?   COMMENT

WHO?   WHEN?   COMMENT